THE FUNNIEST VILLA QUOTES... EVER!

Also available

The Funniest Liverpool Quotes... Ever!

The Funniest Chelsea Quotes... Ever!

The Funniest West Ham Quotes... Ever!

The Funniest Spurs Quotes... Ever!

The Funniest Arsenal Quotes... Ever!

The Funniest Man City Quotes... Ever!

The Funniest Newcastle Quotes... Ever!

The Funniest United Quotes... Ever!

The Funniest Celtic Quotes... Ever!

The Funniest QPR Quotes... Ever!

The Funniest Everton Quotes... Ever!

The Funniest Leeds Quotes... Ever!

The Funniest Rangers Quotes... Ever!

Mad All Over: The Funniest Crystal Palace Quotes... Ever!

Fergie Time: The Funniest Sir Alex Ferguson Quotes... Ever!

I Am The Normal One: The Funniest Jurgen Klopp Quotes... Ever!

I Didn't See It: The Funniest Arsene Wenger Quotes... Ever!

Zlatan Style: The Funniest Zlatan Ibrahimovic Quotes!

'Arry: The Funniest Harry Redknapp Quotes!

War of Words: The Funniest Neil Warnock Quotes!

Chuffed as a Badger: The Funniest Ian Holloway Quotes!

THE FUNNIEST VILLA QUOTES... EVER!

by Gordon Law

Printed in Europe and the USA.
ISBN: 9781696984195
Imprint: Independently published

Contents

Introduction..6

Call the Manager..9

Field of Dreams..19

Lifestyle Choice..31

Boardroom Banter...41

Game For a Laugh..53

Managing Just Fine...61

Calling the Shots..81

Talking Balls...93

Can You Manage?..101

Introduction

As one of the game's biggest personalities, Ron Atkinson always raises a laugh among fans with his outspoken approach.

With his sharp wit and liking for nonsensical football terms, Big Ron was always going to thrive as a football co-commentator.

The former manager was just as entertaining at Aston Villa, where he was the master of a rehearsed quip or biting riposte.

Fast forward a couple of decades and boss Tim Sherwood also calls it as he sees it and enjoys giving wacky responses to the press.

Another ex-manager Martin O'Neill is famous for his energetic antics on the touchline, along with a memorable rant or a quirky observation.

John Gregory, Paul Lambert and David O'Leary have also uttered many bonkers statements while in the Villa Park hot seat.

They all had their own interesting opinions about long-serving chairman Doug Ellis, while 'Deadly' Doug was never shy in making his own feelings known.

Stephen Ireland is a player who enjoyed a good old tirade, while the likes of Mark Draper, Stan Collymore and Ugo Ehiogu have come out with daft statements of their own.

Many of their brilliant bloopers can be found in this unique collection of funny Villans quotes and I hope you laugh as much reading this book as I did in compiling it.

Gordon Law

THE FUNNIEST VILLA QUOTES... EVER!

CALL THE MANAGER

"We feel very, very hard done by. No, make that very, very, very, very hard done by."

David O'Leary is still very, very, upset about the referee's performance against Arsenal

"It wasn't a gilet, it was a coat."

Tim Sherwood corrects a reporter on the item of clothing he flung to the dugout after Villa's equaliser against QPR

"You got yourselves into this f*cking mess. You can get yourselves out of it."

Graham Taylor's half-time warning to the team who were 2-0 down at Crewe. Villa ended up winning the tie 3-2

"In terms of finishing fourth, on that performance we wouldn't finish 44th."

Martin O'Neill after Villa's 7-1 thrashing by Chelsea

"At least we were consistent – useless in defence, useless in midfield and crap up front."

Ron Atkinson after a 3-0 defeat at Coventry

"They weren't happy about the penalty but they calmed down a bit when I pointed out theirs was 15 yards offside."

Martin O'Neill after Villa's 1-1 draw against Middlesbrough

"Newcastle should appoint Glenn [Roeder] as manager straight away because with that luck he will win the Premiership."

David O'Leary after Villa lost to Newcastle. Glenn Roeder responded: "I'll say something controversial for once: what David O'Leary said is a bit spiteful. I thought Villa were very lucky to be only 2-1 down at half-time."

"You don't need to be Einstein to tell them what went wrong at Chelsea."

Paul Lambert reflects after an 8-0 thumping

"Our back four were at sixes and sevens."

Ron Atkinson

"Don Hutchison fell over so often I thought he'd borrowed Emile Heskey's roller skates."

John Gregory

"Certainly for someone like him, I'm surprised he knew what a cabbage was."

Steve Bruce is not amused after a fan threw the vegetable in his direction

"I would have choked him! They are fine now... I think."

Martin O'Neill on the clash between Gabby Agbonlahor and Marlon Harewood after Agbonlahor decided not to pass to his teammate against Everton

"The decisions decided a lot of things, but I'll leave other people to decide."

David O'Leary decides to blame the ref after a 3-0 cup defeat at Doncaster

"I tried to have a word with him after the game but he wouldn't speak to me. He's untouchable. He should have been a policeman."

John Gregory on referee Jeff Winter after losing to Leicester

"The people chanting 'Taylor out!' were the ones singing 'Graham, give us a wave' when we were two up at Everton."

Graham Taylor

"You can't print the things I'm feeling."

Under-pressure Paul Lambert after a 5-0 defeat by Arsenal

"The penalty decision put us back in the game. The player should have been sent off, but Mr Harris didn't know who the player was who handled. The ref did get the minute's silence right before the game, though."

John Gregory is upset about the officiating

"We had a very constructive discussion at half-time, then decided to give it the b*llocks."

Ron Atkinson

"It was the best feeling in the world. When I left home my missus said she had done the EuroMillions, £54 million. But I said I would rather have three points all day."

Tim Sherwood after a win over West Brom

"I haven't got the word power of a Wordsworth, Milton or Chaucer, so I just told him he was brilliant."

Martin O'Neill after Emile Heskey scored the winner on his debut

"We were wimpish – and w*nky, like they say in Men Behaving Badly."

John Gregory after a Villa defeat

"We were done by our Achilles heel, which has been stabbing us in the back all season."

David O'Leary on his side's set-pieces

"We f*cked around with it and got what we got, which was a defeat."

Steve Bruce after a 1-0 loss at Blackburn

"I don't think we should have shoot-outs. We should have a shoot-the-ref shoot-out. After that penalty, the referee should have been shot."

John Gregory after Villa gave away a late penalty in their cup shoot-out defeat against West Ham

THE FUNNIEST VILLA QUOTES... EVER!

FIELD OF DREAMS

"Aston Villa have some of the worst players I have seen in my life, that is the truth."

Colombian Freddy Grisales after Villa refused to offer him a deal following a trial

"Do you think we are going to come out on to the pitch next Saturday with machine guns and shoot the England team?"

Turkish international Alpay Ozalan ahead of England's trip to Turkey

"When I joined Villa I didn't know where they played. I thought they were a London club!"

Christian Benteke needs a geography lesson

"They said, well, funnily said: 'We need the money', so that was that really... I could understand if I was getting sold for £200m, it might make sense. But it was a bit strange."

Richard Dunne on why a 'broke' Man City sold him to Villa for a reported £5m

"If I wasn't playing, I'd be putting slates on roofs back in Ireland. Playing has got to be better than that."

Paul McGrath

"The hardest part of captaining that team was tossing the coin and picking up the trophies."

Dennis Mortimer

"Twenty seven years old, choice health, good knees, world-class agent. There was no way I could fail."

Tony Cascarino on his record transfer from Millwall

"I would say it is better to be five points ahead of the bottom three, rather than five points behind."

Patrik Berger

"To be fair, I don't get many bookings, I just get a load of red cards."

Richard Dunne feels hard done by

"I have reached an agreement [to join] an English club, but I cannot say the club's name. Aston Villa know the club's name. I will play for the biggest club in England."

Alpay Ozalan fell out with the club and later had his contract ended by mutual consent. He then joined Korean side Incheon United

"I've only taken one penalty before, for Crystal Palace at Ipswich when it was 2-2 in the 89th minute. I hit the post and we went down that year. But I think I would be far more comfortable now than I was then."

Gareth Southgate before his England v Germany shoot-out miss at Euro 96

"I just feel, I've got the feeling, that I just don't like them. That's just the feeling I get from the whole club and the fans."

Olof Mellberg on Birmingham City

"I would not sign for another club, not even for 15 million dollars. However, it would be different if they were to instead offer me 15 different women from all around the world. I would tell the club chairman: 'Please let me make these women happy – I will satisfy them like they have never been satisfied before'."

Sasa Curcic lays down his terms for a move away from Aston Villa

"I got a text message from the FA saying I was in the England squad. It was too intellectual for a footballer to have written it. All the spellings and the punctuation were correct."

Curtis Davies

"If I had knocked on it I would have probably had it slapped back in my face!"

Zat Knight on why he hasn't been knocking on Martin O'Neill's door for a recall

"I'm sure that people will always say, 'He's the idiot who missed that penalty'."

Gareth Southgate reflects on Euro 96

"The tweet sent out from my account involving a picture of a car was totally accidental it – happened whilst driving and the phone was in my pocket."

Joleon Lescott after angry fans reacted to him posting a photo of a £121,000 Mercedes directly after Villa's 6-0 defeat by Liverpool

"If I was still at Ipswich, I wouldn't be where I am today."

Dalian Atkinson

"I'd like to play for an Italian club like Barcelona."

Mark Draper

"It's Liverpool and if I was in Gareth's position I would go there tomorrow. It is the opportunity of a lifetime in my opinion. I would go to Liverpool and experience it."

Patrik Berger tells Villa teammate Gareth Barry to join Liverpool – the Czech was soon shown the door

"I'm as happy as I can be – but I have been happier."

Ugo Ehiogu

"There's never a lot of Brazilian football played in these games."

Gareth Barry on Midlands derby matches

"I know almost every player by name already. I play a lot of Championship Manager and Gareth Barry is always a good buy. Hopefully he is just as good in real life."

Joey Gudjonsson on arriving at Villa

"I hopped in the taxi to Glasgow airport with one thought in my mind – where on earth was Aston Villa?"

Andy Gray on signing for the club

"I have accepted that the remainder of my career will be at smaller clubs. Aston Villa is perfect for me."

Martin Laursen charms the Villa faithful

"Someone asked me last week if I miss the Villa.
I said, 'No, I live in one'."

David Platt on moving to Italian side Bari

"The chance that I will now sign for Aston Villa
is almost zero. I don't like to be messed about.
You can write down that this transfer is now off."

Ron Vlaar ended up joining two weeks later

"National teams don't interest me. I have more
to do than go off for three days to play Andorra.
And when you are Irish, you are well aware
you'll never win the World Cup."

A grumpy Stephen Ireland

THE FUNNIEST VILLA QUOTES... EVER!

LIFESTYLE CHOICE

"Nobby smells nice and I hope many people buy it. I hope my teammates buy it – the dressing-room smell now is bad: Nobby is better."

Nolberto Solano has a new perfume 'Nobby'

"I had more different women than I scored goals. And I scored 23 goals."

Gary Shaw reflects on the 1980/81 title-winning season

"My addictions are always there, waiting there for me. They're doing press-ups outside my door."

Paul Merson

"I didn't realise until recently there was a game called Championship Manager. There's people up all night doing this and then they drop you a letter and want to know why you haven't signed Jimmy McHagen from Real Sociedad. When in actual fact Jimmy died four years earlier. And then you could have got him for £2.5m when his price on the thing was £6.5m. It's great."

Martin O'Neill

"Early on, one of the guys posed me a question: 'Ereyergoinfersumscran?'. I later understood that this was a polite invitation to go for lunch."

Brad Friedel

"I guess life is quite mad. I think Monty Python got it spot on. Life is like a Monty Python sketch; men dressed up as women exploding all over the shop. I think that's quite true to life."
John Gregory

"You wonder if this city will ever run out of grey paint."
David Ginola on living in Birmingham

"I had shortish hair when I came here but I couldn't speak any English and so I couldn't go to the hairdresser to tell him what I wanted done."
Juan Pablo Angel on his long locks

"It was a large oversight on his behalf and the players think he should have been fined double. I used to do it myself – not lap dancing, there weren't such things in my day."

Martin O'Neill after John Carew was seen in a lap dancing club hours before a UEFA Cup tie

"I do know her through a friend but I'm not giving her one."

Lee Hendrie on Big Brother's Jade Goody

"I couldn't even spell blog and my children are incredibly embarrassed that I couldn't open... what do you call it... a computer."

Martin O'Neill the technophobe

"What the f*ck is art? A picture of a bottle of sour milk lying next to a smelly old jumper? What the f*ck is that all about? And look at opera. To me it's a load of sh*t. But people love it. I'd say football is art. When I watched France v Holland at Euro 2000, I was orgasmic."

John Gregory

"When I went for a haircut in Dublin, I asked for a Valderrama and they gave me a Val Doonican."

Andy Townsend

"Although I love it, I'm hopeless at golf. My handicap? Severe."

Martin O'Neill

"What's it like at Sellafield? Not too bad I don't think. You don't get people walking down the street glowing. I've had a few comments about that, but it's not that bad."

Scott Carson grew up near the nuclear site

"I like Quentin Tarantino films and stuff like that. There's nothing better than a good bit of violence."

Mark Draper

"The accelerator's position meant my right knee was giving me grief."

Alan Wright on why his £50,000 Ferrari had to be sold

"Delphy pulled up with a brand new Range Rover and was showing it off to the lads. While he was talking sh*t, I sloped off to the kitchens and got the chef to deliver a lovely big brown trout. With Delphy's back turned, I shoved it under the driver's seat and we set off as a team for Norwich... He got back, opened the car door and was nearly sick. I had about 12 voicemails from him, saying he'd had to drive home with his head out the window, retching, and was cursing the good Given family name."

Shay Given pranks Fabian Delph

"I am Welsh and people shout 'sheep' at me, that sort of thing."

Mark Delaney

"I play a bit of snooker myself and I watch quite a lot, but that isn't why I was named as I am. Unfortunately I've never met Steve Davis the snooker player, I've only seen him on TV."

Steve Davis

"[Gerard] Houllier asked me to come and live in Birmingham because it was taking me 75 minutes to come to training... For a start, Birmingham is a crap city and I wasn't going to make the effort, especially as I wasn't playing... I don't give a damn for Ireland. Live in Cork? I'd rather shoot myself. I prefer Los Angeles."

Stephen Ireland

THE FUNNIEST VILLA QUOTES... EVER!

BOARDROOM BANTER

"The way we played left me feeling humiliated and embarrassed... It was more painful to lose against Doncaster Rovers than having my neck broken, which I spent 17 days in the Priory hospital with. It was the worst performance for years."

Doug Ellis

Steve Stride: "Can I introduce you to Kevin Costner?"

Doug Ellis: "Hello Keith, what job do you do?"

Kevin Costner: "I'm an actor Mr Ellis."

When Doug Ellis met Kevin Costner in the Villa boardroom

"Having finally stayed up, I went to see Villa's chief executive [Paul Faulkner] and said, 'I'll have a report on your desk tomorrow morning outlining exactly what we need for next season'. He just looked back at me with a pair of big puppy eyes and I thought, 'Right, I'll go and clear my desk instead'."

Alex McLeish

"AVFC is unique. So will Villa Park go away and become the Doritos Bowl? That is not going to happen."

Randy Lerner comforts the supporters

"The trouble is that the chairman thinks we're like Manchester United, but acts small. We have to put up with that. He thinks we're the only club in the area and that everybody has to support Aston Villa. He's stuck in a time warp. We're dragging him, kicking and screaming into the millennium."

John Gregory on Doug Ellis – he later had to apologise for the statement

"When [Bosko] Balaban came back after the summer, I said, 'Oh, you're back'. He said, 'You remember me then?' I said, 'With the money I paid for you, I'll never forget you, my son'."

Doug Ellis on the £6.7m striker

"My way of handling 'Deadly' was by and large to ignore him. I didn't see any need to pop into the ground every day for a cosy chat. As a result I would get a deluge of memos and faxes. Those of relevance I attended to. The rest went in the bin."

Ron Atkinson on Doug Ellis

"You can't compete when Arabs have a well of oil that gushes at the bottom of their garden."

Doug Ellis

"Only women and horses work for nothing."

Doug Ellis on awarding himself a pay rise

"When Tommy [Docherty] does his rounds of after-dinner speaking, he uses me at every opportunity. Greavsie [Jimmy Greaves] calls me 'Deadly' and lads in the street shout, 'Oi, Deadly!'... If you operate at a high profile, you have to accept criticism."

Doug Ellis on the price of fame

"Not sure what Mr Gold is after other than publicity. When you get down in the mud and wrestle with a pig, the pig loves it... and you get muddy."

Director Charles Krulak on Birmingham chairman David Gold's bid to cut ticket prices by 20 per cent

"Apparently he [Xia] is in the dressing room getting the lads a pizza. He wants to be picked next week and he's got his wish! Anything he wants he can have – it's his club! I spoke to him yesterday and I'll go and enjoy a cup of tea with him now – green tea, Chinese tea. Apparently he's in the dressing room looking for me – I better run!"

Steve Bruce after his first meeting with owner Dr Tony Xia

"This is my life. I kick every ball and sign every cheque. They'll carry me out of here in a box."

Doug Ellis

"Quotation from Mao: 'We must have faith in the masses!' Truly fans' viewpoints are even better than scouting reports!"

Dr Tony Xia's views on having fans as scouts, using a quote from Chairman Mao Zedong, who is believed to be responsible for more than 40 million deaths

"Ron Atkinson is one of the top three managers in the country."

Doug Ellis – he sacked him five days later

"I will never sack another manager."

Doug Ellis in 1997 – before three managers 'resigned'

"How many of you know who this is?"

Silence greets Doug Ellis in the press room at the unveiling of new manager Josef Venglos

"Get the ball in the bloody net, that's what I want."

Chairman Fred Normansell's simple instructions to new boss Jimmy Hogan

"The chairman, Doug Ellis, said he was right behind me. I told him I'd sooner have him in front of me where I could see him."

Tommy Docherty after being sacked

"Their intelligence, across the board, is a lot higher than in my day. Comic Cuts was the typical newspaper of the dressing room, whereas now it's the serious papers. We actually got complaints that there was only one public phone in the changing rooms because they wanted to ring their stockbrokers after training."

Doug Ellis

"Mr [Randy] Lerner was pleasantly surprised that I knew some things about American football, though he may have suspected I'd done a bit of homework the night before."

Martin O'Neill on the Villa chairman who formerly owned the Cleveland Browns

"To be fair, although there's been 11 Villa managers in roughly 30 years, there's only been seven I've sacked."

Doug Ellis

"Well, it's a love-hate relationship – and he loves me."

Graham Taylor on 'Deadly' Doug Ellis

"You don't get this at Birmingham City."

Doug Ellis on a violin virtuoso by Nigel Kennedy at the club's AGM

THE FUNNIEST VILLA QUOTES... EVER!

GAME FOR A LAUGH

"I was just awful. I didn't contribute anything. I've been bigging myself up, saying I'm ready and obviously I'm not. I'm honest with myself in every performance and that was rubbish – I looked like a pub team player."

Curtis Davies on his Villa debut

"As the first bars ring out, I notice the TV camera starts to zoom in. Should I move my lips and sing the two or three lines that I know?"

Andy Townsend on singing the Irish national anthem

"I'm on top of the moon."

Lee Hendrie after his England debut

"I'm sure I'll be a laughing stock in Birmingham for the next couple of weeks."

Peter Enckelman hopes his bizarre own goal against Birmingham will quickly be forgotten

"It was dangerous. Someone tried to take my boot off. People tried to kiss me and were biting me. It was scary."

Fabian Delph on a pitch invasion in the FA Cup win over West Brom

"I got the ball and the crowd started singing, 'One Ronnie Corbett...'."

Alan Wright

Journalist: "Any comment, David?"

David Ginola: "No – I'm too fat."

Ginola, who was branded overweight by John Gregory, responds with a goal and fine performance against Man City

"My mum won't half be pleased."

Nigel Spink to manager Tony Barton as he prepared to take the place of Jimmy Rimmer eight minutes into the 1982 European Cup Final

"I took a whack on my left ankle, but something told me it was my right."

Lee Hendrie

"We were playing away and we'd taken this 15-year-old apprentice with us. As was the custom, a whisky bottle was passed round. Players took a drink, then when they'd gone on to the pitch, Vic Crowe took a big swig. The apprentice asked him why and he replied, 'Son, when you're manager of this club you'll know why'."

Jim Gumbes

"So sorry to every Villa fan after that appalling display. I'm embarrassed to call myself a footballer after that rubbish, sorry."

James Collins after Villa's 7-1 thrashing by Chelsea

"It is a very sad day for English football. Players get stick all the time from the fans, but it seems you cannot have a go back these days."

Mark Bosnich after giving a 'Nazi' salute to Spurs fans

"I will have to sit down and think about my next move. I don't know if I can get a World Cup place if I'm not playing for Villa."

Emile Heskey's high self praise

"I didn't say I want to quit Villa or anything like that."

Erm... Heskey suffers with amnesia as he appears to back-track days later

"The keeper came off his line and said to me, 'You English pig, you English pig', trying to put me off. I said, 'You get back on your line Fritz and I shall endeavour to knock your square head into a round one'. And the ball shot just past him on the way in, hit the stanchion then almost got him again as it came out."

Eric Houghton on his spot-kick against a German side during pre-season

Interviewer: "There was talk over January that you might be moving somewhere else."

Gabby Agbonlahor: "I think the papers like to chat a load of sh*t, really."

The striker turns the air blue on live TV

THE FUNNIEST VILLA QUOTES... EVER!

MANAGING JUST FINE

Q: "Are you looking to sell any players this summer?"

Graham Taylor: "The big question is: 'Does anybody really want them?'"

"You're always just one defeat from a crisis. On that basis, we're in deep sh*t."

John Gregory

"You've got 25 to 30 babies with dummies ready to come out any time for various reasons. It's about giving them TLC, tender loving care, in their different ways. They've all got different pains."

David O'Leary

"My team won't freeze in the white-hot atmosphere of Anfield."

Ron Saunders

"We've got a young squad and I want to add some experience. And that's why I've signed a 20 and a 21-year-old. I clearly don't know what I'm talking about, do I?"

Martin O'Neill

Journalist: "What was your highlight of the tournament?"

Ron Atkinson: "Bumping into Frank Sinatra."

The Villa boss was a pundit during the 1994 World Cup

"How can anybody call this work? People in the game don't realise how lucky they are. You drive to the ground, play a few five-a-sides, then have lunch."

Ron Atkinson

"The gods are conspiring against us. I think I've shot an albatross or something."

Alex McLeish on Villa's bad run of form

"Referees should be wired up to a couple of electrodes. They should be allowed three mistakes – then you run 50,000 volts through their genitals."

John Gregory

Journalist: "Do you think you'll still be around when you're Dick's age, 67?"

Tim Sherwood: "When your dick's out, did you say? Haha. I hope so..."

The manager laughs at the reporter's pronunciation of the word 'age' when talking about Dick Advocaat

"I enjoyed the occasion last week. Actually, what am I talking about?"

Martin O'Neill on the Carling Cup final defeat by Man United

"I don't want my back four playing football."

Ron Saunders

Journalist: "Martin, have you made any New Year resolutions?"

Martin O'Neill: "Yes I have – and most of them involve you."

"There are no problems if we had to play Eric [Lichaj]. Andy Weimann is champing at the door too."

Alex McLeish. The door?

"All I can say is that there is a train in the distance – and it is not going to stop. It is going to hit you right in the face."

David O'Leary playing with trains

"I don't know if a threat from a teenage girl is much of a threat."

Paul Lambert on death threats Gabby Agbonlahor received from One Direction fans over a charity-game tackle on Louis Tomlinson

"I just panicked."

Graham Taylor explains why he signed Ian Ormondroyd

"We spent enough money, we just bought the wrong players."

Former assistant manager Allan Evans on the 1997/98 campaign

"They are talking about the players going on strike? Well ours have been since Christmas."
Ron Atkinson on a run of goalless games at the beginning of 1992, while the PFA threaten strike action

"I've told the players never to believe what I say about them in the papers."
Graham Taylor

"The fans wanted Ginger Spice in basque and suspenders. I gave them Norah Batty in wrinkled stockings."
John Gregory on working with limited finances

"The chairman of Brighton wouldn't recognise Gareth Barry if he was stood on Brighton beach in the team strip, with a seagull on his head and a ball in his hand."

John Gregory refutes the claim that Brighton made Barry the player he is today

"We're going to put [Barry] Bannan in a grow bag. This is something we've been working on. Fellaini is about 15ft 6in and Barry's 3ft 4in – but we're hoping it works."

Paul Lambert on trying to thwart Everton's Marouane Fellaini. It didn't as he scored in Villa's loss

"Every good team has a strong centre. I'd look round. Goalkeeper, Jim Cumbes. I'd think, 'What time did you get in last night?' Centre half, Chris Nicholl. In the toilet putting his contact lenses in. Central midfield, Bruce Rioch. Shaking like a leaf. Centre forward, Sammy Morgan. Next to Chris putting his contact lenses in. What chance did I have?"

Vic Crowe

"The 1982 team's position in history is well and truly entrenched and I'm sure they will say it will take this team four-million light years to get near them."

Martin O'Neill has probably given up hope of Villa winning the European Cup again

"I look forward to hearing from the silent majority."
Alex McLeish on fans calling for his head

"It would be great if we could put a load of kennels alongside the training pitch to put the players in afterwards. Luxury kennels, take them out, feed them at 9am, train them at 10. Get them back out after lunch and then back in the kennels and keep them there."
David O'Leary

"As I see it, if you're going to commit suicide, you don't do it yourself."
Ron Saunders

"I was having a bite to eat with my daughter yesterday and I dropped a pint of blackcurrant and lemonade all over her. For a young lady that's not very good, it sticks everywhere. She was head-to-toe in it and I thought, 'Wow, my luck is still going'. I'm going to pour a pint of blackcurrant and soda all over her next week. It's going all over her head! Whatever it takes to change the luck. Amy, you're in trouble next week."

Steve Bruce after claiming his first victory of 2017 against Derby

"Sometimes I wish they would cause me a bit of aggro really!"

David O'Leary on his mild-mannered side

"That's as ridiculous a statement as he's made –
and he's made a few in his time."

**Martin O'Neill after Arsene Wenger accused
Villa of being a long-ball side**

"There's something curious about the relationship
between Coventry and Villa. We don't particularly
dislike them. But blimey, do they hate us!"

John Gregory

"Playing for a big club comes with pressure.
Anyone can do it for a lesser team – but you have
to have b*llocks to play for Aston Villa. This is a
big club."

Tim Sherwood

"We've got people at Aston Villa who like wearing dresses and having their bottoms spanked, so Paul [Merson] should fit in well."

John Gregory

Gary Lineker: "You were the man who signed Stan Collymore for Aston Villa – do you view that as a mistake now?"

Brian Little: "No, not yet."

"They are getting in because of a lack of numbers, not because of brilliance."

David O'Leary does not think highly of his young stars

Q: "How would it feel if Villa were relegated?"

Tim Sherwood: "My summer holiday with my kids would not be good – I'd be throwing them in the deep end."

"Allegations are all very well but I would like to know who these alligators are."

Ron Saunders

"Doug [Ellis] insisted on coming on the coach with us, and as we approached Hillsborough, he moved away, joking he didn't want to be hit by a stray sniper's bullet."

Ron Atkinson on his return to former club Sheffield Wednesday as Villa manager

"Even the name [Aston Villa] is beautifully symmetrical, with five letters in each word."

John Gregory

"There is no quick fix – unless we can get a Russian in!"

David O'Leary can't guarantee instant success

"I remember playing against them [Ossie Ardiles and Ricky Villa] in their first game because I scored our goal and played absolutely brilliantly. I outshone Ossie without a doubt. But I'd outshine Ozzy Osbourne as well."

Martin O'Neill displaying the utmost modesty

"It's out of my control now. I'll just turn my phone off."

Tim Sherwood when asked if he feared for his job in his final press conference

"Villa have amazing support. If you hung 11 Villa shirts on a washing line 5,000 fans would turn up to watch them!"

Tommy Docherty

"Referees act almost like policemen, and the fourth officials are becoming jobsworths. They are reporting managers up and down the country for stepping outside the technical area."

John Gregory

"I've never been on a charge before and I'm looking forward to going down there and seeing what the [FA's] premises are like!"

David O'Leary after Villa were accused of making an illegal approach for Saints striker James Beattie

"I don't want angels in my team – they can get out of their brains every night as long as they're man of the match on Saturday."

John Gregory

"If I was going to lie to you, honestly I would lie."

Paul Lambert speaks the truth on why he axed Darren Bent

"I don't want to say anything – not even 'no comment'."

Ron Atkinson on being linked with Liverpool's Dean Saunders

Roy Keane: "It's disgraceful. I've seen him doing it to other managers – it is a disgrace. The game is still going on."

Journalist: "Do you perceive Mourinho to be disrespectful and arrogant?"

Keane: "What do you think? That's a stupid question."

Assistant manager Keane is unimpressed Jose Mourinho approached him and boss Paul Lambert to shake hands shortly before the end of a 3-0 defeat at Chelsea

THE FUNNIEST VILLA QUOTES... EVER!

CALLING THE SHOTS

"Whenever I see his wife, I go out of my way to plant a kiss on both cheeks, which isn't a hardship really because she's a pretty girl."

Graham Taylor on his efforts to get Juan Pablo Angel to stay at the club

"He gets a bit excitable when things aren't going his way. That is probably why he is on nine bookings because he can't tackle a fish supper!"

Steve Bruce on Henri Lansbury

"He's having an indifferent time... People are shouting 'Useless de la Cruz' at him."

David O'Leary on poor old Ulises de la Cruz

"There was a mishap on the training ground. It's a common occurrence between players but on this occasion, unfortunately, it was between the manager and a player."

Martin O'Neill on a fracas with Nigel Reo-Coker

"He used to be fit as a butcher's dog, but now he looks more like Mr Blobby."

John Gregory on David Ginola

"I think [his specialist] got a magic wand out – Paul Daniels his name was."

Tim Sherwood on Idrissa Gueye's speedy recovery from injury

"He's even started swimming, would you believe? He's not very fond of it, but he's trying. It's not a very pleasant sight when he's in the swimming pool I have to tell you, but he's trying like a beast! I had to come out because it was that embarrassing. I had to throw him a floater."

Steve Bruce on Gabby Agbonlahor's fitness programme

"The situation with Alpay is ridiculous. My message to any club is don't be stupid, don't be silly over the price. But for God's sake, somebody pick up the telephone!"

Graham Taylor is keen to get rid of Alpay Ozalan

"The way Ashley Young is built, he looks like a heavy shower could kill him."

Martin O'Neill on Ashley Young

"Stress is a player at Rochdale with a family to bring up and a contract expiring at the end of the season."

John Gregory on Stan Collymore's admission to the Priory for stress

"I always make sure I write 'Atkinson D' on the team sheet. Sometimes I wonder if I'm making a mistake."

Ron Atkinson questions his selection of Dalian Atkinson

"I've said to him, 'I wish I was you, Stan. I wish I was on the money you're earning. I wish I had your lifestyle. And most of all, I wish I had your talent because with it, I'd have been the first name in the England team'."

John Gregory on Stan Collymore

"Lee Hendrie is Lee Hendrie and he always will be."

David O'Leary

"I don't want to go over the top. But with Fabian Delph – there's not a better midfielder in the country at the moment."

Tim Sherwood. Not going over the top?

"Any player judged a failure in the first team is likely to find himself among the reserves at Preston on a wet Wednesday evening. That includes Stan."

John Gregory with another Collymore swipe

"He has put on weight. He'll soon be up to three-and-a-half stone. He is so slim we could put him through a letterbox."

Martin O'Neill has now beefed up Ashley Young

"I know Cyrille [Regis] has found God. Now I want him to find the devil."

Ron Atkinson

"He got a bit homesick for Glasgow – which is a bit strange considering he's a Bulgarian."
Martin O'Neill on Stiliyan Petrov settling at Villa after his move from Celtic

"I just bumped into Cyrille [Regis]. I said, 'What's all this about finding God? You worked with him at West Brom for four years'."
Ron Atkinson on being reunited with the born-again Christian

"You talk about Ronaldo and Messi. Is Young in that company? Yes. I've just put him in it."
Martin O'Neill makes a huge statement on Ashley Young

"His goal wasn't an answer to me, he just wanted to show off his nice slim figure afterwards. He looked alright. He asked me 'Who is this Mr Blobby?'"

John Gregory had labelled David Ginola 'fat' before his goal against Man City and the winger celebrated by taking his shirt off

"[Gabby] Agbonlahor is not quick. But he's fast, very fast."

Graham Taylor

"Some days he could climb Everest, others he can't even climb out of bed."

John Gregory on Stan Collymore

"If I'd had a gun I'd have shot him."

John Gregory after Dwight Yorke stated his desire to join Man United

"He's such an honest person it's untrue."

Brian Little on Ian Taylor

"His left foot is so good he could open a jar of pickles with it."

John Gregory on Steve Staunton

"He's 28 going on 18. The problem is, nobody can be 18 forever, not even Peter Stringfellow."

David O'Leary on Lee Hendrie

"Darius [Vassell] tried to get the blood out himself, which he now realises was not really advisable."

Graham Taylor says his striker was sidelined after drilling a hole in his toe to burst a blister

"I wasn't invited. It's an invite I'd rather not have because they'd want me to foot the bill!"

Dean Smith on Jack Grealish's dinner dates with John McGinn

"Daley could start the game or maybe he'll be sitting on the plank... that's if Dalian doesn't mind."

Ron Atkinson jokes about Dalian Atkinson on Tony Daley's return to action

THE FUNNIEST VILLA QUOTES... EVER!

TALKING BALLS

"He had his head bandaged up the other week after going in where it hurts. Mind you, that was probably the best thing with his dodgy haircut!"

Curtis Davies on Martin Laursen's barnet

"We often played golf together and he always beat me. Then one day I won for the first time. Two weeks later, I was sold."

Chris Nicholl on Ron Saunders

"Even my girlfriend says sometimes, 'Can you be like Christian, he's sweet'. That's the funny part of it. He can be very cute."

Leandro Bacuna on Christian Benteke

"At the moment I am having very difficult moments. I don't play and my coach at Aston Villa has not said, 'Good morning' to me since the start of the season."

Mustapha Hadji on David O'Leary

"He handled the pressure brilliantly during our poor spell – except when he smashed the physio's bag across Goodison Park."

Gareth Southgate on John Gregory

"I got the impression that he didn't much like football."

Jim Cumbes on Ron Saunders

Journalist: "What's wrong at Aston Villa?"

Eric Djemba-Djemba: "I think it's the manager, because the manager needs to change the team... If he doesn't try to do something, maybe we will go to the first division."

David O'Leary called Djemba-Djemba in for a 'chat' before dropping him for the next game

"The gaffer told me the hardest pass is over five yards."

Ashley Westwood on Paul Lambert

"He made me captain by saying, 'Right, you lead 'em out'."

Dennis Mortimer on Ron Saunders

"David O'Leary thinks only of himself and doesn't care about anyone else. It's just him, him, him... The way he has treated me was worse than a dog."
Mustapha Hadji after leaving for Espanyol

"I have two dogs of my own and I know how well they are treated. I wouldn't mind their lifestyle myself."
O'Leary replies to Hadji

"Gilly – next time you speak to the wierdo [sic], tell him to let me go."
Gavin McCann on 'weirdo' Martin O'Neill in a text to his agent Tony McGill

"I played with Ron in about a 100 reserve games. And according to Ron, he was man of the match in 99 of them."

Dennis Jackson on Ron Atkinson

"He invented the banana shot. Trouble was, he was trying to shoot straight."

Ron returns the compliment

"People see you in a certain way and put you in a bracket of, 'Right, he's an a*sehole' and they bracket you there."

John Terry is not an a*sehole

"At Villa, [Ron Atkinson] used to organise some games in training by saying, 'Right, let's have the c*ons against the rest'. We loved it, because we'd always win; on my team would be players like Tony Daley and Dalian Atkinson. No one was offended, because it was just Ron being Ron. He wasn't being racist. He was just having a laugh."

Paul McGrath

"He was one of the biggest pr*cks I have ever had the misfortune to come across."

Stan Collymore on playing under Villa manager John Gregory

THE FUNNIEST VILLA QUOTES... EVER!

CAN YOU MANAGE?

"I could try acting. I could sit down and make little notes and everyone would say I've matured. But I know that's impossible."

Tim Sherwood on his touchline emotions

"Sometimes the gap between a genius and an idiot is wafer-thin. I've seen both sides of it."

Alex McLeish on his Villa tenure

"One thing I took this job for was to prove that David O'Leary doesn't need money."

David O'Leary is out to prove himself, speaking in the third person

"I've not had to ask permission from Geraldine to take the job. I'm one of the few men in this life who are not under the thumb. I'm stronger than that. Did she want me out of the house? Listen, she's wanted me out of the house for the past 27 years and has often asked me not to come back again. But I always show up, and really, she can't do without me, because I'm brilliant."

Martin O'Neill on taking the Villa job

"I understand the fans complaining. They wanted a big name and got me."

John Gregory

"I'll never be able to achieve what Tommy Docherty did and take Aston Villa into the Third Division and Manchester United into the Second Division."

Ron Atkinson

"The more you lose, the more you don't win."

Alex McLeish

"I've been called a stupid Paddy over the years. You've just got to ignore it."

David O'Leary telling Lee Hendrie how to deal with insults

"I think I can be a leader of men, but you're not born with that attitude. In the maternity ward, it's not girls, boys and natural leaders. You have to become that."

Tim Sherwood

"I realise expectations are pretty high. I'm petrified!"

Martin O'Neill after joining the club

"The only way I'd be interested in the England job is as player-manager."

Ron Atkinson

"I don't think I'll ever calm down. I'm afraid that's me. Honestly, I'll just take one massive big 'woof' and I shall be gone. Heart – gone!"

Martin O'Neill on his touchline antics at Chelsea

"So I didn't come in here all guns blazing or wanting to be their headmaster. You can't get personal these days, get your hair cut, and all that nonsense. You've got to move with the times. I left the stick at home, and the tickling brush. Now I feel I know them a bit better. Some get a whack, others a tickle."

Tim Sherwood on his management style

"I've been used to being called Potato Head by them for 20 years and Fathead at Liverpool or whatever."

Steve Bruce laughs about the abuse he previously suffered from Villa fans

"I'm a foreign manager. I'm French. With another manager I'm sure it would be different."

Gerard Houllier hits back at rival bosses

"Would I be any good as a manager? Yes, I'd be brilliant. My ego thinks I'd be good at it and the rest of me thinks I would be brilliant too."

Martin O'Neill on taking the England job

THE FUNNIEST VILLA QUOTES... EVER!

Printed in Great Britain
by Amazon

48884373R00068